HALF TRUTHS
Youth Study Book

Half Truths:
God Helps Those Who Help Themselves
and Other Things the Bible Doesn't Say

Half Truths
978-1-5018-1387-0
978-1-5018-1388-7 *eBook*
978-1-5018-1389-4 *Large Print*

Half Truths: DVD
978-1-5018-1392-4

Half Truths: Leader Guide
978-1-5018-1390-0
978-1-5018-1391-7 *eBook*

Half Truths: Youth Study Book
978-1-5018-1398-6
978-1-5018-1399-3 *eBook*

Half Truths: Youth Leader Guide
978-1-5018-1400-6
978-1-5018-1401-3 *eBook*

For more information, visit www.AdamHamilton.org.

Also by Adam Hamilton

24 Hours That Changed the World

Christianity and World Religions

Christianity's Family Tree

Confronting the Controversies

Enough

Final Words from the Cross

Forgiveness

John

Leading Beyond the Walls

Love to Stay

Making Sense of the Bible

Not a Silent Night

Revival

*Seeing Gray in a World of
     Black and White*

Selling Swimsuits in the Arctic

Speaking Well

The Call

The Journey

The Way

Unleashing the Word

When Christians Get It Wrong

Why?

ADAM HAMILTON

Author of *24 Hours That Changed the World, The Journey,* and *The Way*

HALF
TRUTHS

GOD HELPS THOSE WHO HELP THEMSELVES AND OTHER THINGS THE BIBLE DOESN'T SAY

Youth Study Book
by Mike Poteet

Abingdon Press / Nashville

HALF TRUTHS
Youth Study Book

Copyright © 2016 by Abingdon Press
All rights reserved.

This book is printed on elemental chlorine-free paper.

ISBN 978-1-5018-1398-6

16 17 18 19 20 21 22 23 24 25 —10 9 8 7 6 5 4 3 2 1
MANUFACTURED IN THE UNITED STATES OF AMERICA

CONTENTS

INTRODUCTION

Everybody knows that in the classic movie *Casablanca*, Humphrey Bogart says, "Play it again, Sam."

Except he doesn't. (He really says, "Play it, Sam.")

Everybody knows that one of Captain Kirk's most famous lines in the *Star Trek* series is "Beam me up, Scotty."

Except he never says it. (He comes close once, in the movie *Star Trek IV*—"Scotty, beam me up"—but that was in 1986, after "Beam me up, Scotty" had a been a pop culture mainstay for twenty years.)

Everybody knows that Sherlock Holmes likes to say, "Elementary, my dear Watson."

Except the great detective never says that, not once in any of Sir Arthur Conan Doyle's fifty-six short stories and four novels about him. (Holmes says one or the other half of the line a number of times, but never together.)

In the same way, there are a lot of things that "everybody knows" the Bible says. Except sometimes it doesn't.

The Bible never says, "Everything happens for a reason." Or "God helps those who help themselves." Or "God won't give you more than you can handle." The Bible also never claims to be the direct and unmediated Word of God. And it never says that Jesus told us, "Love the sinner, hate the sin."

All these ideas are half truths that creep into many Christians' faith. The problem is not so much that the statements are wrong as that they're just not

1

quite right enough. Taken at face value, and taken to extremes, they can lead to mistaken beliefs about God, Jesus, and our fellow human beings. Wrong beliefs can lead to wrong practice.

Wrong beliefs can also prove painful. Many times, we tell people these things with nothing but the best of intentions. We fully intend to love our neighbor by offering helpful and comforting words. But because these words aren't fully true, they can end up causing a lot of damage. The words might cause other people, if they have faith, to stumble in their beliefs. If the other people don't have faith, these half truths might prove a roadblock in their ever coming to faith. And, in either case, these statements might damage relationships. If you say something hurtful to someone, even when you didn't mean to, that person may be less likely to stay connected to you going forward, for fear she or he will be hurt again.

In this study—based on Adam Hamilton's book *Half Truths*—you will examine some half truths . . . things that "everybody knows" the Bible says, except it doesn't. You'll discover what each half truth gets right and what it gets wrong. By the time we're done, maybe you'll have a better handle on what Scripture really leads us to believe and do, and how to live as a truthful disciples of the one who promised his Spirit would lead us into all truth, Jesus Christ.

1.

EVERYTHING HAPPENS
FOR A REASON

*[Then Moses said to the Israelites,] "I call heaven and earth to
witness against you today that I have set before you life and death,
blessings and curses. Choose life so that you and your descendants
may live, loving the Lord your God, obeying him, and holding fast
to him; for that means life to you and length of days."*
—Deuteronomy 30:19-20a NRSV

Gather Around God's Word

Lead me in your truth—teach it to me—because you are the God who saves me.
I put my hope in you all day long.

(Psalm 25:5)

3

Open the Bible and light a candle.

God of truth, we admit your ways often seem hidden from us, and we confess we often claim more knowledge of your will than we actually possess. May your Spirit guide us to humbly seek signs of your work. Help us place less trust in our own wisdom and more trust in your Son, Jesus Christ, who became wisdom from you for us, to make us righteous and holy and to save us. Amen.

Sing or read "Be Still, My Soul" (words by Katharina von Schlegel)

Jesus said, "You are truly my disciples if you remain faithful to my teaching. Then you will know the truth, and the truth will set you free." (John 8:31-32)

Jesus said, "I am the way, the truth, and the life. No one comes to the Father except through me." (John 14:6)

Getting Started

Spend some time browsing recent issues of your local newspaper or a magazine focused on current events and/or some local, national, and world news websites. Clip or copy two or three headlines that grab your attention. Spread them before you and look at them as you think about these questions:

- Which, if any, of these headlines make sense to you? Which ones agree with your understanding of how the world works, or ought to work?
- Which, if any, of these headlines leave you shaking your head and asking why?
- In which, if any, of these headlines do you think you see glimpses of God at work? Why?
- What do you imagine Jesus would say if he were reading these headlines with you?

Study the Scripture

Read Deuteronomy 30:11-21. Moses is addressing the Israelites at the end of their forty years of wandering in the wilderness, just before they enter the land God has promised them as their new home.

- In your own words, what is Moses' main message to the Israelites? What does he want them to do?

- What reasons does Moses give for the Israelites to do what he is telling them? (See especially verses 11-14, 16.)
- What consequences will the Israelites face if they fail to do what Moses tells them? (See especially verses 17-18.)
- In your experience, how easy or difficult is it to do what Moses is telling the Israelites to do? Can you talk about a time when you either did or did not make the choice Moses wants them to make? What happened?
- Do you think Moses' message accurately explains why we experience "blessing and curse" (verse 19)? Why or why not?
- How much freedom do you think God gives us to choose what we do and what happens to us? Explain your answer.

Read and Reflect

Do We Choose Our Own Adventures?

In middle school, my favorite books were the *Choose Your Own Adventure* series. In these books, "you" are the hero—sometimes an ordinary kid in such extraordinary circumstances as a haunted house or a lost civilization; sometimes someone more exotic like an astronaut, secret agent, or circus performer. "You" start reading on page 1, but what pages you turn to next depends on how you respond to various decision points in the text.

Some choices are pretty routine stuff: "If you go west, turn to page 5. If you head east, turn to page 13." But other choices seem more consequential. Will you trust the mysterious wizard to lead you out of the cave? Turn to page 29. Will you tell the unidentified alien ship that you welcome it in peace? Turn to page 42.

I never felt really satisfied unless I got to make at least a dozen choices before hitting those dreaded words in bold face at the bottom of the page: The End (usually preceded by "your" sudden, terrible demise).

Choose Your Own Adventure books can be a lot of fun, but the series title is a little misleading. Sure, you make decisions that affect how you read the plot—but the book's author has determined in advance all the choices and their consequences. Everything that happens in these books, including every single forced choice the reader makes, is put there for a reason—the writer's reason, not yours.

Thankfully, in real life we really get to "choose our own adventures," right? While none of us have completely blank pages handed to us at birth—we can't control where or to whom we're born, for example, or whether we're born in good health—we're more or less free to make our own choices and write our life stories for ourselves. Aren't we?

Not if you believe this half truth Christians often say they believe: "Everything happens for a reason."

What This Half Truth Gets Right: God Cares and God Rules

People often tell this half truth to themselves and others when everything is going badly—*really* badly. A loved one dies. A storm does terrible damage. A job is lost. "It's sad and terrible," they'll say, "but, even if we can't understand it now, we have to believe it happened for a reason."

This half truth is what theologians call a *theodicy* (*thee-ODD-ih-see*), a defense of God's goodness and power in the face of what could be evidence to the contrary.

Try and think about the following three statements, all of which Christians claim are true, all at once:

1. God is all-loving.
2. God is all-powerful.
3. Suffering exists.

If all these statements are true, how can an all-loving, all-powerful God let suffering happen?

- Maybe God *is* all-loving but not powerful enough to stop our suffering. But is a god who is powerless against suffering the God we read about in the Exodus, or in stories of Jesus healing sick people?
- Maybe God *is* all-powerful but doesn't really love us, meaning God is content to let us suffer. But Scripture shows us a God whose love leads to the relief and ultimate end of suffering. (For example, see the description of God's promised future in Revelation 21:4.)
- Maybe suffering is an illusion. That conclusion seems to fly in the face of millennia of human experience, but at least it keeps God's hands clean. Some world religions do teach that suffering isn't real, but classic Christianity never has taught that—how could it, when Jesus suffered and died?

No single theodicy satisfactorily juggles all three of those statements at once. And, as theodicies go, "Everything happens for a reason" is better than some.

It avoids two big theological mistakes: atheism, which claims there is no god, and deism, which affirms God's existence but claims that God took a "hands-off" approach to the world once God finished creating it.

The idea that "everything happens for a reason" agrees with biblical teaching that God cares about and stays involved with the world. It's really a statement about God's providence. Here's something you can impress your teachers with: The word *providence* comes from the Latin prefix *pro*, "before," and the verb *video*, "to see." God sees what is best for us, and provides accordingly.

If you had been a young Protestant Christian in sixteenth-century Germany, you might have had to memorize and recite this definition of God's providence:

> The almighty and ever present power of God by which God upholds, as with his hand, heaven and earth and all creatures, and so rules them that leaf and blade, rain and drought, fruitful and lean years, food and drink, health and sickness, prosperity and poverty—all things, in fact, come to us not by chance but by his fatherly hand. [1]

There's no question the Bible teaches about God's providence. The psalm-singer praises God for feeding people and wild animals alike (Psalm 104). Jesus said if God can be trusted to give birds food and wildflowers beauty, then God can also be trusted to give us what we need (Matthew 6:25-32). But do "all things" come to us *directly* from God's hand? Is random chance really never at work? Does God actually choose who will get good weather and who will get bad, who will grow rich and who will stay poor? Does God ever cause bad things to happen?

What This Half Truth Gets Wrong: It Can Paralyze Us and Hurt Others

If we press this view of providence too far, we end up with a god who looks less like a loving parent and more like a *Choose Your Own Adventure* writer. If "everything happens for a reason" in a divinely micromanaged way, then we *aren't* really free, and our choices *don't* really matter, because God has already plotted our lives down to the last page.

A belief that God has plotted our lives and everything else for a reason could suck a lot of wind out of our sails.

- Why study for that algebra test? God has already decided if you'll get an *A* or an *F*.

- Why work up the nerve to ask that good-looking girl or guy to prom? If God has picked out a soul mate for you, she or he will show up when God is good and ready.
- Why should fast-food employees demand a higher minimum wage? God has already determined their earning potential and place in life.
- Why should we race for cures, wear rubber bracelets, and issue ice bucket challenges to raise money for disease research? Whether you make it through life with a clean bill of health is up to the divine doctor, isn't it?

If we're not careful, the idea that "everything happens for a reason" can leave us paralyzed and passive before a god who's holding all the cards, who moves us around like characters in a book for purposes unknown and unknowable.

Besides paralyzing us, the saying can hurt others. Does the tragic death of a parent or sibling or friend really "happen for a reason"? In using this saying to help friends who are suffering, we can inadvertently cause them pain, because these words seem to imply that God caused the tragedy, that God manipulates us like chess pieces for unknown purposes. Because of this implication, using the saying with friends might actually damage their faith in a time when they need it most.

Beyond theodicy, beyond logic, beyond definitions, Christ calls us to love. When we use the half truth "Everything happens for a reason," there's a possibility that instead we will hurt others.

Really Choosing God

Deuteronomy 30 gives us another way of thinking about God's providence. The Israelites, who used to be slaves in Egypt, are about to enter the Promised Land. Moses tells them they have a serious decision to make: they can choose to obey God and build their community according to God's will *or* they can choose to go it alone, ignoring God's guidance, following make-believe gods in hopes that those gods will bring blessing. One choice leads to life; the other, to death.

Moses urges the Israelites to choose life by choosing God. God has seen what is best for God's people and has provided; God has freed them and brought them to a new home. But God hasn't robbed them of their ability—their *responsibility*—to make choices that matter.

God's commandments aren't arbitrary rules designed to make life less fun. They show us how we are most likely to experience God's goodness: by worshiping God, by telling the truth and keeping our promises, by respecting and loving our neighbors. When we make these kinds of choices, choices that line up with God's priorities and values, we're more likely to choose adventures in which we "live and thrive" (Deuteronomy 30:16), as God wants us to.

Of course, choosing these adventures isn't as simple as turning to one page instead of another. Godly choices don't always lead immediately to good outcomes; think of the martyrs throughout Christian history—and even today, in some parts of the world—who lose their homes, their jobs, even their lives because they remain faithful to God. And not all people who suffer bring it on themselves. Sometimes wrong choices affect other people more than they do the person who made them; sometimes bad things do happen by chance.

God doesn't make everything happen for a reason—but God can bring meaning out of anything that happens. "We know," wrote the apostle Paul, "that God works all things together for good for the ones who love God, for those who are called according to his purpose" (Romans 8:28). Nothing that happens, and no choice we make, can ultimately derail the great adventure God has chosen for us and for all creation, because "nothing can separate us from God's love in Christ Jesus our Lord" (Romans 8:38).

Suggested Activities

1. It's a Good Thing/Bad Thing

Play this improvisational performance game with a partner: One of you starts the game by announcing some crazy, make-believe event (for example, "My neighbor's house was swallowed by a dinosaur last night"). Your partner gives a reason why the event was a good thing ("That's good; now the dinosaur won't go hungry"). You respond with a reason why it was a bad thing ("But now my neighbor has no place to live"). Your partner responds with another positive ("Your neighbor can move wherever she wants to"); you respond with another negative ("But the dinosaur will follow her wherever she goes")—and so on, and so on . . . the more outrageous, the better.

- How is this game like and unlike people trying to determine why and whether "everything happens for a reason"?

9

2. Watch a Movie

Signs (Touchstone Pictures, 2002; directed by M. Night Shyamalan) is about a former pastor, Graham (played by Mel Gibson), who discovers mysterious crop circles on his farm. Soon, strange lights start appearing in night skies around the world. Graham struggles not only to protect himself and his family from extraterrestrial invaders but also to make sense out of confusing, unresolved events from his past and present.

In one scene, Graham tells his brother: "See, what you have to ask yourself is, what kind of person are you? Are you the kind who sees signs, sees miracles? Or do you believe that people just get lucky?"

- Which kind of person do you tend to be? Why?
- What answers, if any, does this movie give to the question, "Does everything happen for a reason?" Do you agree with its answers? Why or why not?

3. Plot a Personal Timeline

On a separate piece of paper, plot some major events of your life on a timeline. Illustrate it if you wish, with sketches or photos. Now modify your timeline in these ways:

- Draw a square around events you had no control over.
- Draw a diamond around events that were shaped, to some extent, by your choices; above or below those events, jot down notes about the choice you made, why you made it, and what you imagine might have happened had you made different choices.
- Draw a cross at those points, if any, when you were confident you felt God's guidance.
- Draw a question mark at those points, if any, when you were less sure of God's presence.

If you feel comfortable doing so, talk about your timeline with a Christian friend you trust.

4. Make a Mobile

Mount headlines and pictures clipped from newspapers and magazines to circles and squares cut from construction paper. Cut various lengths of string or yarn; tape one end of each length to the back of the construction paper and tie the loose ends to a wire coat hanger. Experiment with adding and removing paper clips to the construction paper in order to make the mobile as balanced as possible.

- How do you think your mobile might be an image of how God is at work in the events of our world and our lives?

Daily Bible Readings

Day 1: Genesis 3:1-13

Some people argue that God is ultimately responsible for human sin. Why did God put a forbidden tree in Eden in the first place? Didn't God *know* Adam and Eve would eat its fruit? Do you think God is somehow to blame for what happened? What does this story tell you about human beings' freedom and responsibility to make choices?

Day 2: Job 2:1-10

Job accepted all his suffering as "from God" (verse 10)—patiently in these verses, but not so much in most of the book! Can we thank God for the good in our lives without also blaming God for the bad? Have you ever demanded God tell you why bad things happen, as Job demands in the rest of the book? What happened?

Day 3: Ecclesiastes 9:1-12

The author of Ecclesiastes didn't believe that "everything happens for a reason" but did write a lot about how random chance and death affect everyone, good or bad. What do you think of his advice for living? Can you believe that some things "just happen" and at the same time believe that Jesus' resurrection changes our attitude toward death?

Day 4: Luke 13:1-5

The people around Jesus want to find a deeper meaning in Pontius Pilate's murder of people as they worshiped at the Temple. Jesus rejects their conclusion about this event, as well as another one—a tower's sudden collapse—and says the people should draw a different lesson. What choice does Jesus say tragedies and disasters like these should motivate people to make?

Day 5: John 9:1-7

People in Jesus' day often assumed a direct link between personal suffering and sin. How does Jesus challenge this commonly made connection in the case of the man born blind? Do you think Jesus' words in verse 3 mean that God *caused* the man's blindness or *used* it? Why? When have you seen personal hardships (your own or someone else's) bring glory to God?

Day 6: Romans 8:26-39

How can each of the truths that the Apostle Paul discusses in these verses encourage us as we think about the mystery of why things happen: The Holy Spirit's prayers for us? God's ability to make all things work for good? God's knowing, calling, and saving us? The strength of God's love for us in Jesus Christ?

2.

GOD HELPS THOSE
WHO HELP THEMSELVES

*The helpless commit themselves to you; you have been the helper of
the orphan.... O LORD, you will hear the desire of the meek; you
will strengthen their heart, you will incline your ear to do justice for
the orphan and the oppressed.*

—Psalm 10:14b, 17-18a NRSV

Gather Around God's Word

Make your ways known to me, LORD; teach me your paths.

Lead me in your truth—teach it to me—because you are the God who saves me.

(Psalm 25:4-5)

Open the Bible and light a candle.

God of truth, you command us to practice the pure and spotless religion of helping other people in their distress. By your Spirit, strengthen us to hear your call to serve and to respond, believing that when we help those who are helpless, we are helping your Son, Jesus Christ, who helped while we were still sinners, giving his life that we might live. Amen.

Sing or read "Grace Alone" (Scott Wesley Brown and Jeff Nelson, © 1998 Maranatha! Music)

Jesus said … "You are truly my disciples if you remain faithful to my teaching. Then you will know the truth, and the truth will set you free." (John 8:31-32)

Jesus answered, "I am the way, the truth, and the life. No one comes to the Father except through me." (John 14:6)

Getting Started

- Sit in a straight-backed chair with your feet flat on the floor and your arms folded across your chest so that your hands are on your shoulders. What happens when you try to stand up without leaning forward?
- Place your hand on a table, fingers splayed (as though you were going to trace your hand). Fold your middle finger backward so that it is touching your palm. Raise and lower your thumb. Raise and lower your index (pointer) finger. Raise and lower your pinky. What happens when you try to raise and lower your ring finger?

These situations should leave you helpless—unable to do what is asked of you—but only temporarily and in a very specific way.

When is a time when you have *really* felt helpless? What did you do about it? What happened?

Study the Scripture

Read Psalm 10.

- What is the psalm-singer's complaint?
- What evidence does the psalm-singer cite that supports this complaint?

- How does the psalm-singer want God to respond?
- Describe the shift in the psalm-singer's attitude from the beginning of the psalm to its end. Why do you think this shift happens?
- Talk about a time when you felt, as the psalm-singer does, that God was standing far off. How did you handle that experience?
- How comfortable are you expressing feelings of helplessness to God in prayer?
- What Bible stories can you think of that support the psalm-singer's words to God, "You do see troublemaking and grief, and you do something about it!" (verse 14)?
- How have you personally experienced God helping you or someone you know?
- What people in your community need help so that they "will never again be terrified" (verse 18)?
- Bible scholars say Psalms 9 and 10 are probably meant to be a single psalm. How does Psalm 9 apply Psalm 10's lessons about how God helps, from individuals to the lives of whole nations? How do you think nations today need to remember and respond to the truth that real help comes from God?

Read and Reflect

Bart Simpson, Theologian?

Hard as it may be to believe now, when *The Simpsons* debuted in 1989 it was controversial. Well-meaning grownups wrung their hands about how it would corrupt America's youth. I remember my pastor denouncing from the pulpit one episode that he believed mocked common decency in general and Christian faith in particular.

In the episode, the Simpsons are hosting Homer's boss for dinner. Homer desperately wants his family to make a good impression. He asks Bart—the rebellious kid best known at the time for telling people to "eat my shorts"—to say the mealtime grace. Bart folds his hands and bows his head, then prays, "Dear God, we paid for all this stuff ourselves, so thanks for nothing."

My pastor was scandalized, but I thought the scene was funny. Because, let's face it—Bart has a point. God didn't do the grocery shopping. Human beings made the meal happen. Maybe you personally didn't do anything to get your food today, but plenty of other people did. Farmers grew the grains, harvested the produce, raised the animals. Truckers moved goods to processing plants and grocery stores. Someone purchased and prepped what's on your plate. So why give God a shout-out?

We thank God because, in the psalm-singer's words, God "make[s] grass grow for cattle...[and] plants for human farming in order to get food from the ground" (Psalm 104:14-15). God gave us life and a world capable of sustaining it. When Jesus taught his disciples to pray for their daily bread, he wasn't teaching them that God makes food show up by magic. He was teaching that, whenever we help ourselves to food, we're only able to do so because God helped us first.

All blessings flow from God, but frequently they flow through a divine-human partnership. That's the truth Bart Simpson's prayer can teach us.

The All-American Half Truth

The truth Bart Simpson can teach us, however, has been cut in half. It's become a saying so familiar that over 75 percent of American teens think it's a Bible verse: "God helps those who help themselves."[2]

This half truth has been part of the United States' religious thinking since our nation's beginning. As a result, we tend to place a premium on people helping themselves. Although the sentiment predates Christianity, we have Benjamin Franklin to thank for its widely known form. He put it in *Poor Richard's Almanac*,[3] his collection of pithy proverbs that offered eighteenth-century readers what we might today call "life hacks," hints for happiness and success.

As practical advice goes, this half truth isn't all bad. Even before Franklin, early Americans had discovered its value. One example: The winter of 1609–1610 was bitter for English colonists in Jamestown, Virginia. Food was scarce during "the Starving Time." Recent archaeological excavations revealed that settlers even resorted to eating dogs, cats, horses—and at least one dead fourteen-year-old girl.[4] (Did your American history teacher ever tell you *that*?) To give the colony a shot at survival, its leader, Captain John Smith, decreed, "[Y]ou must obey this now for a Law, that he that will not work shall not eat."[5] Smith's law echoed a rule the Apostle Paul laid down for an early Christian congregation: "If anyone doesn't want to work, they shouldn't eat" (2 Thessalonians 3:10). The experience could be considered a case study in the practical benefit of believing that "God helps those who help themselves."

What This Half Truth Gets Right:
Personal Responsibility

You're probably not facing any circumstances as dire as those faced by the colonists in Jamestown. But you may be in situations where simply waiting around for God's help isn't the best option.

- God *could* miraculously grant you better grades on your report card—but regular attendance, completed homework, and hard studying are all better bets.
- God *could* make a college acceptance letter or a job offer fall from heaven—but, honestly, you won't go to the school of your choice or get the work you want without submitting applications.
- God *could* give you perfect health and a fit physique while you sleep—but making healthy food choices and exercising regularly are surefire ways to get into shape.

People who wait around for God to act without acting themselves are like the folk in Dr. Seuss's *Oh, the Places You'll Go!* who are stuck in "The Waiting Place," where *nothing* happens because no one is *making* anything happen. Everyone is depending upon someone or something else to take the initiative...or even just for something to occur at random...or for some vague undefined something that may never come at all. They're waiting "perhaps, for their Uncle Jake / or a pot to boil, or a Better Break." And as they wait, they forget that—to paraphrase Seuss—God gave us brains in our heads and feet in our shoes, to steer ourselves any direction we choose.[6]

I like what one denomination's statement of faith says about human existence: "Life is a gift to be received with gratitude and a task to be pursued with courage."[7] If you have big dreams and grand plans, by all means pray about them—but don't expect God to hand you results wrapped with a shiny bow in response. You are responsible for *doing* something about what you want your life to be. Get out there and help yourself!

What This Half Truth Gets Wrong:
God, Helper of the Helpless

Unfortunately, this half truth leads us in the wrong direction when we assume that God *only* helps people who help themselves. The Bible consistently witnesses to a different truth: God *especially* helps people who *cannot* help themselves.

Psalm 10 is one of many biblical texts celebrating God's help for the helpless. We don't know who first sings this psalm, but he or she feels under attack from more powerful foes. Enemies are laying traps and plotting not only against the psalm-singer but also against society's most vulnerable members: people in poverty, children without parents, all those on the social sidelines whose lack of money and influence means their protests against corruption and injustice go unheard. These "helpless victims are crushed," the psalm-singer laments; "they collapse, falling prey to the strength of the wicked" (Psalm 10:10).

But there is hope! The psalm-singer believes God will make things right: "You do see troublemaking and grief, and you do something about it!" (verse 14). God will "listen closely" to the victims of wickedness, and will "establish justice for the orphan and the oppressed" (verse 18).

Plenty of people who are poor show up in Scripture, but the Bible spends little time wondering how they became poor or what they should do about it. "Thou shalt get a job" isn't one of the Ten Commandments, and "Blessed are they who pull themselves up by their own bootstraps" isn't one of Jesus' Beatitudes. What the Bible *does* talk about is how God helps people who are poor, sick, orphaned, weak, or in any way left to fend for themselves on the margins.

God "gives justice to people who are oppressed...gives bread to people who are starving...frees prisoners...makes the blind see...straightens up those who are bent low...protects immigrants...helps orphans and widows...[and] makes the way of the wicked twist and turn!" (Psalm 146:7-9).

What's more, the Bible talks a lot about how God wants to send this help to the helpless *through us*.

Will God Love Them Through Us?

Let me tell you about another pastor from my youth, who worried about something a lot more substantial.

Our congregation's big, historic building was downtown in a major city. Many members lived in nicer parts of town, or even in the suburbs, and drove downtown for worship and other activities. Not many, my family included, lived near the church's immediate neighbors who dealt with poverty, crime, homelessness, drugs, and other familiar urban challenges.

An opportunity came for the church to buy a vacant building next door and transform it into a community services center. Some on the church board were skeptical. There were so many other things, things the church needed or wanted, that the money could be spent on. And serving free meals every now and then to people in poverty was fine, but getting involved with them in-depth, in an ongoing way—providing food and clothing and shelter but also literacy classes, job training, medical care—well, was the church really called to make all that happen?

I didn't see it for myself, but I'm told my pastor listened quietly to all the objections raised by the board members around the table, then leaned forward, peered at them intently over the top of his glasses, and said, "God is going to love this city. The only question is, Will God love this city through us?"

The plan passed, and even today that church is a leader in providing emergency and ongoing assistance to people who cannot help themselves.

Whenever we help people who cannot help themselves, we reflect and spread the love of God: "God shows his love for us, because while we were still sinners Christ died for us" (Romans 5:8). God is gracious, which is another way of saying God helps the helpless, including you and me. God "brought us to life with Christ while we were dead as a result" of our sins—"You are saved by God's grace!" (Ephesians 2:5). God saves us by grace, not only for an eternity in God's presence but also for a life, here and now, of helping those who cannot help themselves.

Suggested Activities

1. Acrostic Poetry

Bible scholars point out that in the original Hebrew, Psalms 9 and 10 were probably a single psalm. The combined psalm is a loose acrostic poem: every second poetic line (except in 10:3-6) starts with a letter of the Hebrew alphabet, moving through the alphabet from start to finish (but some letters are missing). Write your own acrostic poem about how you have experienced God's help, and ways you have helped or plan to help others in response. Use the letters of your name, or a meaningful word or phrase, as the basis for your poem; or follow the psalm-singer's lead and use all or a portion of the alphabet.

2. Illustrate a Story of God's Help

Scripture has no shortage of stories about God helping people who cannot help themselves. Select one of these stories to illustrate—write and draw a comic book, make a diorama, paint a watercolor. Whatever medium you choose, clearly show how God's help made a difference. Some stories to consider:

- God makes a promise to Hagar (Genesis 16)
- The Israelites cross the Red Sea (Exodus 14)
- God sends manna in the wilderness (Exodus 16)

- Daniel in the lions' den (Daniel 6)
- Jesus stills a stormy sea (Mark 4:35-41)
- Jesus helps the woman accused of adultery (John 8:1-11)

3. Connect with a Helping Ministry

Get involved, if you aren't already, with some ongoing ministry or program that offers help to people who need it. Your youth ministry and congregation may already support such programs; you could also look outside your congregation to community assistance programs, local charities, and so on. Commit to helping for more than one or a few occasions; pick a program you can stick with for some time. Keep a journal or blog/vlog about your experiences. What new things did you learn about how to help people?

4. Watch a Movie

The Soloist (2009, rated PG-13) is based on the true story of journalist Steve Lopez (played by Robert Downey Jr.) who meets a former Juilliard music student, Nathaniel Ayers (Jamie Foxx), who has become homeless; Nathaniel lives under a Los Angeles freeway, playing the violin. Steve decides he will try to help Nathaniel improve his life.

- How does Steve try to help Nathaniel? What do you think about Steve's motivations?
- Do you think Steve ends up helping Nathaniel? Why?
- How does Steve say Nathaniel ends up helping him?
- In what ways does this film define and illustrate the meaning of grace?
- What lessons can Christians learn from *The Soloist* about what helping people means and looks like in practice?
- Do you think *The Soloist* affirms or challenges the idea that "God helps those who help themselves"—or does it do some of each? Explain.

Daily Bible Readings

Day 1: Psalm 121

Bible scholars think ancient pilgrims on their way to worship at the Temple in Jerusalem would sing this psalm as they prepared for the long journey up Mount

20

Zion. How have you experienced God helping you during the "pilgrimage" that is your life? In what ways has God protected you?

Day 2: Exodus 14:10-18

The story of the Exodus, the fundamental story that shaped ancient Israel's faith, is all about God helping people who could not help themselves. How do experiences of God's help involve both staying still (verse 14) and being on the move (verse 15)? How does helping the helpless bring glory to God?

Day 3: Leviticus 19:1, 9-10

For ancient Israel, being "holy" didn't mean being "holier than thou." Holiness meant doing things that marked Israelites as radically different from others, set apart for a special purpose. How do these laws about harvesting crops mark ancient Israel as holy? What are some modern practices that you think are equivalent to leaving the harvest's leftovers to help those who are hungry?

Day 4: John 15:1-5

Why does Jesus use the metaphor of a vine and its branches to describe his relationship to his disciples? What "fruit" have you been able to produce because of your connection to Christ? Have you ever experienced for yourself the truth of his words, "Without me, you can't do anything" (verse 5)? What happened?

Day 5: James 1:22-27

For the apostle James, true religion is a matter of correct action, not simply correct belief (see 2:19!). Widows and orphans were some of first-century society's most vulnerable members; they are still often among the most vulnerable today. What other people in your community are in special need of help? How will you and your youth ministry or congregation help them?

Day 6: Romans 5:6-11

God did not wait until we could help ourselves to help us in Jesus Christ! What are the results of God's acts for us in Jesus, according to the Apostle Paul? This week, how will you reflect your "restored relationship" with God (verse 11) in acts of helping others?

3.

GOD WON'T GIVE YOU
MORE THAN YOU CAN HANDLE

*No temptation has seized you that isn't common for people. But
God is faithful. He won't allow you to be tempted beyond your
abilities. Instead, with the temptation, God will also supply a way
out so that you will be able to endure it.*

—1 Corinthians 10:13

Gather Around God's Word

Make your ways known to me, LORD; teach me your paths.
Lead me in your truth—teach it to me—because you are the God who saves me.

(Psalm 25:4-5)

23

Open the Bible and light a candle.

God of truth, you don't willingly afflict anyone, and you shower your compassion over all that you have made. When we face any kind of temptation or trouble, may your Spirit move us to look to and trust in you, for you have shared and overcome human suffering in your crucified and risen Son, Jesus Christ. Amen.

Sing or read "How Firm a Foundation" (from Rippon's Selection of Hymns, 1787)

Jesus said…"You are truly my disciples if you remain faithful to my teaching. Then you will know the truth, and the truth will set you free." (John 8:31-32)

Jesus [said], "I am the way, the truth, and the life. No one comes to the Father except through me." (John 14:6)

Getting Started

How long can you…

- Run in place?
- Stand in one place?
- Keep a blown-up balloon in the air by batting it around?
- Do a crab walk?
- Spin in a circle without falling down (or making yourself sick!)?

Write down your times, compare them with someone else's—and get ready to think about some more serious forms of endurance.

Study the Scripture

Read 1 Corinthians 10:1-13.

- According to Paul, what experiences and other things united the freed Israelite slaves as they left Egypt (verses 1-4)? (You might want to check out Exodus 13:21-22; 14:19-22; 16:14-15; 17:5-7.)
- Paul's talk about the Israelites being "baptized into Moses" (verse 2) and drinking from Christ (verse 4) only make sense when we know Paul is telling the Exodus story with *typology*, where one thing is a "type"—a model, a pattern—of something that follows

it later. Why does Paul want his early Christian readers to connect with the Israelites, and how does typology help him make that connection?

- Paul reminds his readers that God judged the people in the wilderness. (You might want to check out Numbers 14:1-25; 21:5-6; 25:1-9.) Why was God angry with the people? What does Paul want his readers to learn from the Israelites' wilderness experience?
- What has happened that makes Paul think he and his readers are those "to whom the end of time has come" (verse 11; see 15:20-28)? How does Paul think this sense of urgency about the future should shape Christian behavior? Do you think Christians two thousand years after Paul's day can share that urgency? Why or why not?
- What kind of caution does Paul urge in verse 12? Has there ever been a time in your life when you've seen what Paul is warning about happen to someone (including, maybe, yourself)? What happened?
- What good news does Paul give people who are facing temptation?
- How do you handle feelings of temptation? What or who has been God's "way out" of temptation for you (verse 13)?

Read and Reflect

Big-Time Bible Blunders

Have you ever noticed a typo in a book you're reading? Did you circle and correct it, or just let it slide?

What would you do if you caught a typo in the *Bible*?

It's happened! In fact, collectors of old and rare books have nicknames for some of history's best-known botched Bibles.

- "The Vinegar Bible"—Published in 1717, the heading on one page calls Jesus' parable of the vineyard (Luke 20:9-19) the "parable of the vinegar."[8] I'm sure the printer felt bitter regret. (Sorry, I couldn't resist.)
- "The Judas Bible"—This 1613 edition mistakenly says, in Matthew 26:36, that *Judas*, not *Jesus*, went with his disciples to Gethsemane.
- "The Wicked Bible"—This 1631 Bible commands readers, in Exodus 20:14, "Thou shalt commit adultery." (Oops!)

You know how your Language Arts teacher is always telling you to proofread your essays? *This is why!*

(On the other hand, typos might pay off. The "Wicked" Bible's printers had to pay a fine and destroy as many copies as they could,[9] so only ten copies are known to still exist. One of the copies, at auction, recently sold for over $47,000.[10])

I wonder whether this session's half truth—"God won't give you more than you can handle"—began as a simple but significant misreading of a Bible verse. It basically misquotes 1 Corinthians 10:13, which says God won't let us *be tempted* beyond our ability to handle *the temptation*. But somewhere along the line, those bits about temptation dropped out. Maybe some first-century Christian youth group was playing a game of "Telephone" with the Apostle Paul's letter; who knows?

Whether somebody skipped a few words or just misunderstood Paul's point, a promise about God's loving faithfulness turned into a very different kind of statement—a "theological typo" that Christians, definitely shouldn't let slide.

Tempting, Isn't It?

Paul was writing to believers in Corinth to clear up some of their questions. They were new to faith in Jesus (of course, in the first century every Christian was) and they faced the disadvantage of trying to follow Jesus faithfully in one of ancient Greece's most famously beautiful but also notoriously sinful cities. All the temples and statues in Corinth honored the gods of Mount Olympus, not the God of Israel, the God and Father of the Lord Jesus. Idol worship ran rampant in Corinth. Its tendrils snaked into so many aspects of everyday life, it was hard to ignore—and all too easy to make moral compromises with.

Food, for example. Want to eat? (Most folks do.) In ancient Corinth, you had to buy your meat in the public marketplace, like everyone else. Trouble was, you had no way of knowing whether the meat you bought came from animal sacrifices to idols. Sure, *you* would know "a false god isn't anything in this world" (1 Corinthians 8:4)—but if you ate meat that was dedicated to false gods, would you somehow be giving a little approval to idol worship? What if a fellow believer who was less mature in faith happened to see you chowing down, and it rattled him so badly he started to waver? In that case, "the weak brother or sister for whom Christ died is destroyed by your knowledge" (8:11). Paul said he'd rather go hungry than give in to the temptation to eat sacrificed meat.

Or consider the fact that sex was a big part of worshiping idols. Having sex with temple prostitutes was a way of communing with the divine; at least, that's what the highly ritualized, super-secretive cults in Corinth taught. Christians knew better—or were supposed to. But some Corinthian Christians were visiting temple prostitutes, a habit that, in some cases, opened the door to more sexual immorality; one man was "having sex with his father's wife" (5:1). Sexual temptations can be hard to resist, but Paul didn't think many in the congregation were even trying.

And so Paul retells the Exodus story to the Corinthians. He reminds them that many of the freed Hebrews abused their freedom to indulge themselves, defying God and grumbling against God's goodness. "God was unhappy with most of them, and they were struck down in the wilderness" (10:5) and never saw the Promised Land. Paul urges his readers to learn from their spiritual ancestors' mistakes and to resist all temptations to ungodly behavior.

What This Half Truth Gets Right:
God Knows We Have Limits

That's where the *whole* truth behind this session's half truth comes in. Paul reassures the Corinthians that he's not setting some impossibly high behavioral bar for them. "God is faithful," Paul tells them, and "won't allow you to be tempted beyond your abilities. Instead, with the temptation, God will also supply a way out so that you will be able to endure it" (10:13).

Paul tells the Corinthians the temptations they're wrestling with, as serious as they are, are nothing new. Food, sex, money—these things have always proved potential pitfalls. But Paul's larger point is this: When we feel the most pressure to give up on God, *just then* God refuses to give up on us! God provides a way for us to escape temptation. We have only to look for and take it!

- Maybe we stop to pray when we feel tempted.
- Maybe we remove ourselves from circumstances where temptations are around.
- Maybe we confide in a fellow believer or seek a professional's help.

Whatever form our escape route may take, it's a gift from God.

Although this half truth has forgotten that Paul was talking about temptation, it manages to get God's faithful concern for us right. God doesn't want to watch us crash and burn when we face life's trials. Instead, God promises to help us through them. As God said through the prophet Isaiah, "When you pass through the waters, I will be with you....When you walk through the fire, you won't be scorched..." (43:2).

What This Half Truth Gets Wrong: God Doesn't Pile On

Unfortunately, there's a *major* problem in saying, "God won't give you more than you can handle." The inevitable implication is this: God is giving you tough stuff to deal with in the first place.

At its core, this half truth shares the same flawed premise we saw in the first half truth we looked at, "Everything happens for a reason." As we saw then, while God can certainly *use* anything that happens to us, God doesn't necessarily *cause* everything that happens to us—including our suffering. Scripture is uniquely inspired by God, and we should be careful thinking that our hardships, while very real and very painful, are sent from God.

I believe God doesn't give us more than we can handle because God isn't interested in giving us hardship at all. God doesn't "pile on" when we're having hard times, burdening us until just before we reach our breaking point. God doesn't kick us when we're already down. And, no, God doesn't always, or even usually, take away our hardship with a snap of the divine fingers—but God *does* always bear it with us.

We know this because, in Jesus Christ, we meet a God who, so far from dishing out suffering and heartache and pain, takes it all upon God's own self. Jesus "offered prayers and requests with loud cries and tears as his sacrifices to the one who was able to save him from death" (Hebrews 5:7). Jesus knows firsthand what it feels like to be weighed down and overcome with suffering; even as he was dying on the cross, he called out, "My God, my God, why have you left me?" (Matthew 27:46; Mark 15:34). He wasn't playacting—he felt pain in the depth of his soul just as intense as anyone else who's ever prayed a prayer like that. But if God brought Jesus through the darkness of suffering for the sins of the world to a resurrection morning, how much more can God be trusted to bring *us* through *our* suffering? And so the apostle Peter urges his readers, "Cast all your anxiety on him, because he cares for you" (1 Peter 5:7 NRSV).

God gives us a Savior who strengthens us to cope with pain, confusion, fear, sadness, and trouble. Instead of giving us more than we can handle, God gives us a Savior who can handle it all.

Suggested Activities

1. Build a Weight-Bearing Structure

Using only drinking straws, pipe cleaners, and paper clips, build a structure that can support a golf ball. In order to successfully complete the challenge, you'll have to experiment to find out how much weight various arrangements of your building materials can bear. (If you want inspiration or hints online, try such sites as "Tall Tower Challenge" at https://www.howtosmile.org/resource/smile-000 -000-003-953.) As you work, think about how *you* must not give your structure more than it can handle—but remember (as Adam Hamilton writes in *Half Truths*) that *God* helps us handle all that we are given!

2. Practice *Lectio Divina*

Lectio divina is a Latin phrase that means "divine reading." It is a way of reading Scripture that focuses on making ourselves open and receptive to the way God uses a particular passage to speak directly to us. There is no single "right way" to do *lectio divina*; here is one method you can use:

- Sit in a comfortable and quiet space and read Psalm 27 aloud, making a note of a word, phrase, or image that captures your attention; mark it in your Bible or write it down on another piece of paper. Spend a few minutes simply thinking about what you've noticed.
- Now read the psalm again. Where do you see or hear your life connecting with these words? Write about or draw a picture of this connection.
- Read the psalm a final time. What do you sense God calling you to do or to be today in response to this psalm?

3. Watch a Movie Clip

Watch the scene near the end of *The Lord of the Rings: The Return of the King* (2003) where, as Frodo and Sam are almost at the end of the quest to destroy the evil ring of power, Frodo, exhausted and at his breaking point, decides he can't go on.

- How does Sam become Frodo's "way out" of the temptation to give up?

- How might this scene illustrate how God is with us when we are strug-
  gling with burdens of our own?
- How can you "carry" someone who is having trouble enduring difficult
  times?

4. Write an Encouraging Letter

Paul wrote to the Corinthians when he knew that the congregation was
facing temptations. We may not always know when someone is wrestling with
a temptation, but we can often observe when someone is going through tough
times. Write a brief letter of encouragement to someone you know who is
enduring difficult circumstances. (A handwritten letter can communicate a level
of personal warmth and concern that e-mails and text messages can't always
match.) If possible and appropriate, make an offer of practical help in your letter.
Consider quoting an encouraging verse from Scripture.

Daily Bible Readings

Day 1: Isaiah 43:1-4

God spoke these promises through Isaiah to a community—the Jewish exiles
living in Babylon—but we can also read them as promises to us as individuals.
What deep waters or burning fires have you faced (or are you facing) in your life?
Can you sense God's presence with you in those circumstances? How? Why does
it matter that God does not say "if" we face such times, but "when"?

Day 2: James 1:13-18

The Apostle James may have felt that he was correcting a "theological typo" for
his readers. What truths does he tell them about God's character? What "perfect
gifts" has God given you in your life? How do James's words help us when we're
facing times of temptation or trouble?

Day 3: Psalm 77

In the first half of this psalm, the psalm-singer certainly feels as though he or
she is facing more than one person can handle. What happens so that the second

half of the psalm communicates a very different experience? What does this psalm teach us about handling times of sorrow and grief?

Day 4: Hebrews 4:14-16; 5:7-9

How does the truth that Jesus lived a fully human life benefit us when we are being tested or are facing suffering? How confidently do you approach God when you pray? What was a time you found God's grace when you needed help? How did that grace come to you, and how did you respond?

Day 5: 1 Peter 5:6-11

How does remembering that we are not the only people who suffer help us bear suffering? What explanation does Peter give for his readers' suffering? Does it help you make sense of suffering today? Why or why not? What hope does Peter offer his readers?

Day 6: Philippians 4:10-13

What is the Apostle Paul's secret to experiencing contentment in all circumstances? What is something in your life currently for which you need God's strength to help you endure? How can you encourage someone else who needs to endure tough times, as the Philippians encouraged Paul?

4.

GOD SAID IT, I BELIEVE IT, THAT SETTLES IT

Every scripture is inspired by God and is useful for teaching, for showing mistakes, for correcting, and for training character, so that the person who belongs to God can be equipped to do everything that is good.

—2 Timothy 3:16-17

Gather Around God's Word

Make your ways known to me, LORD; teach me your paths.
Lead me in your truth—teach it to me—because you are the God who saves me.

(Psalm 25:4-5)

33

Open the Bible and light a candle.

God of truth, you have promised that your Word does not return to you empty, but achieves the purpose for which you spoke it. By your Spirit, keep us attentive to your living Word, Jesus Christ, that we may discern and do his will, faithfully and joyfully serving and loving others in his name. Amen.

Sing or read "O Word of God Incarnate" (William W. How, 1862)

Jesus said... "You are truly my disciples if you remain faithful to my teaching. Then you will know the truth, and the truth will set you free." (John 8:31-32)

Jesus answered, "I am the way, the truth, and the life. No one comes to the Father except through me." (John 14:6)

Getting Started

What do you think of these quotations from famous people about the Bible?

> I would like so much for all Christians to be able to comprehend "the surpassing worth of knowing Jesus Christ" through the diligent reading of the Word of God, for the sacred text is the nourishment of the soul and the pure and perennial source of the spiritual life of all of us.
>
> —Pope Francis[11]

> [The Bible] is full of interest. It has noble poetry in it; and some clever fables; and some blood-drenched history; and some good morals; and a wealth of obscenity; and upwards of a thousand lies.
>
> —Mark Twain[12]

> [The Bible is] not a book of laws and morals—it's a book of stories, about ordinary, unqualified people doing extraordinary things.
>
> —Madeline L'Engle[13]

> I'm trying to be a Christian and the Bible helps me to remind myself what I'm about.
>
> —Maya Angelou[14]

Study the Scripture

Read 2 Timothy 3.

- Paul's description of what people will be like in "the last days" is rough stuff! (See especially verses 1-5.) How does his advice to avoid such people compare or contrast with Jesus' attitude toward "sinners" in such passages as Mark 2:15-17 or Luke 19:10? Do you think Jesus would agree with Paul's advice to Timothy here? Why or why not?
- Paul also writes that "immature women" will be a particular problem in the last days (verses 6-7). Why does Paul seem to have more to say about the women than the people leading them astray? How do Paul's words here compare or contrast with Paul's teachings in 1 Corinthians 14:33b-35? What about in Galatians 3:27-28? What about Paul's own attitude toward women in working with them as partners in ministry? (He mentions ten such women in Romans 16:1-15, including the deacon Phoebe and the apostle Junia.) Do you sense a tension among these texts and, if so, how do you explain it?
- Who were Jannes and Jambres (2 Timothy 3:8)? What do you make of the fact that their story, clearly known to and regarded as important by Paul and Timothy, is not found in the Old Testament?
- What makes Scripture useful, according to Paul, and for what purposes?
- How have you experienced Scripture's usefulness in one or more of the ways that Paul mentions? How did Scripture help you or someone else do "everything that is good" (2 Timothy 3:17)?
- "Scripture," for Paul, meant what we call the Old Testament. Do you think he would agree that his letters, and the rest of the writings in the New Testament, are also inspired and useful? How do you think the church came to claim that they are?
- Scripture is one tool that Paul tells Timothy to use in order to continue in truth. What other resources does Paul offer?

Read and Reflect

No Cracks About "The Book"?

In an old *Star Trek* episode called "A Piece of the Action," the U.S.S. *Enterprise* boldly goes to a "strange new world" that seems awfully familiar. Captain Kirk and Mr. Spock beam down to a planet where an entire society has patterned itself after Prohibition-era Chicago, ruled by rival, machine gun-wielding mob bosses who fight endless skirmishes over territory.

Watching the episode, we can't help wondering how this culture of gangsters, gamblers, and bootleggers could have developed on a planet thousands of light-years from Earth. The answer, it turns out, is funny. A different earth vessel visited about a century earlier and accidentally left behind a book, *Chicago Mobs of the Twenties*. The planet's natives—"very bright and imitative people," Spock says—adopted this book as a blueprint. Now, a hundred years later, they take its every word as infallible guidance for living, even though it never was intended to be that. The mob bosses even proudly display leather-bound copies on lecterns in their offices. The book has become "The Book," and the planet's people tolerate no questioning of it or speaking against it. "You watch it," one boss cautions Kirk. "The Book tells us how to handle things." Another declares, "I don't want any more cracks about The Book!"[15]

Obviously, "The Book" is a stand-in for the Bible. So is the show simply anti-Scripture? Or is it critiquing how some people read and use—or, perhaps, abuse—the Bible?

In *Half Truths*, Adam Hamilton describes bumper stickers that read, "God said it, I believe it, that settles it." The slogan is a declaration of faith in the Bible's importance and authority. It's meant to affirm Scripture as God's Word. It suggests that the speaker has the final say about the meaning of Scripture and about what Christians should believe and do as a result.

But is the slogan really any of these things? Is it even a biblical sentiment? Or is it as misinformed and misguided as those extraterrestrial mobsters' reverence for "The Book"?

"God Said It"?

The Greek word *biblia* means "books." Though we've brought them together between one set of covers, the books that make up the Bible emerged over thousands of years, from many places. And they are different *kinds* of books: poetry, history, law, letters, even ecstatic visions. If bookstores didn't already have Bible sections, stockers would have a hard time knowing where to shelve this volume.

Parts of Scripture do present themselves as speech from God. The phrase "Thus saith the Lord" shows up over four hundred times in the King James version.[16] But the Bible itself never claims God as its author.

Tradition identifies numerous people as biblical authors: Moses, King David, King Solomon, the four Evangelists, the early apostles. God's people have always understood that Scripture comes from multiple sources. God didn't drop the Bible, fully finished, from heaven. Instead, God used different people, with their different viewpoints and talents—and, yes, their weaknesses and limitations—to write texts that proved themselves, time and again, to be texts through which God continued to communicate with God's people.

In his second letter to Timothy, the Apostle Paul explains God's connection to Scripture this way: "Every scripture is inspired by God…" (3:16). Remember that, for Paul, "scripture" was our Old Testament. Paul certainly believed that he taught and wrote with God-given authority, but he had no way of knowing that later generations of God's people would consider his letters—let alone letters by Peter and John, and the four Gospels, and the book of Revelation—to be Scripture.

Why did Paul's letters come to be considered Scripture? Because later readers recognized that Paul's words, too, were "inspired." *Inspired* means "God-breathed." It's the same action God took with the first human creature: God "blew life's breath" into it, and "[t]he human came to life" (Genesis 2:7). You and I and all people are "inspired" by God—breathed into and made alive—and so, says Paul, is Scripture.

Some religions do claim that God dictated their sacred writings. Muslims, for example, believe the Qur'an is God's direct speech, spoken in Arabic to Muhammad. The Qur'an is translated and read in other languages, but many Muslims who don't already know Arabic learn the language as a religious duty, for then they believe they can read and recite God's exact words.

It's no judgment against Islamic faith to point out that Christians believe the Bible is different. I heard a college professor of religious studies state the contrast accurately and without judgment: "For Muslims, the Word became book. For Christians, the Word became flesh." Christians believe God's Word—God's most direct, most perfect message to humanity—is Jesus.

Does that mean the Bible is "just a book"? Only if we treat it that way. Unless and until we read Scripture in dependence upon God, its words are just ink on the page or pixels on the screen. But when we ask and expect God to inspire our reading and hearing of Scripture, even as God inspired its writing, then we open ourselves to meeting God's living Word, Jesus, through the Bible's written words. In that sense the Bible is indeed "the Word of God"—not God's direct speech written down, but writings that God still reliably uses, as Paul told Timothy, to teach, correct, and train us in faithful living.

What This Half Truth Gets Right:
"I Believe It"

Christians must take the Bible seriously, and this half truth does. It affirms the Bible's authority. Religious scholars frequently classify the world's faiths according to whether they rely on *general revelation* (knowledge about the divine that is self-evident, easily inferred from nature or experience, or otherwise available to everyone) or *special revelation* (knowledge about the divine that depends on a specific, particular person, text, practice, or other source).

We believe that Jesus is God's Word made flesh. We *don't* believe that that was self-evident when he walked the earth—indeed, as the Gospel of John tells us, "his own people didn't welcome him" (1:11). If you want to know who Jesus really was and is, then you must read the Bible. If you want to know about his resurrection on the first Easter, you must read the Bible.

And it's not just Jesus. If you want to know how God saved the people of Israel from slavery in Egypt, you must read the Bible—no clearly explicit reference to the Exodus has yet been found in any other ancient text. Or if you want to know that the God of Israel, the God and Father of Jesus Christ, created the universe, you must read the Bible—science masterfully explains the *what* and *how* of the natural world, but acknowledges it cannot address the *why*.

Christianity is a religion of special revelation, and the Bible is our indispensable record of that revelation. To one degree or other, Christians believe the Bible.

What This Half Truth Gets Wrong:
"That Settles It"

I'll be honest: Even as I typed that last sentence, I could imagine a dozen or more different objections (some of them my own) from a dozen or more different Christians. I imagined some saying, "What do you mean, 'to one degree or other?' You either believe it or you don't; there's no halfway!" I imagined others saying, "Do you mean I have to believe the Bible when it says Joshua made the sun 'stand still,' or that Jonah survived three days after being swallowed by a big fish? How much of this stuff do *I* have to swallow to still be a Christian?"

Even among Christians, then, appealing to the Bible doesn't always "settle" questions. Some Christians believe the Bible is *inerrant*—without any factual mistakes in any of its content, at least in its (now inaccessible) original manuscripts. Others believe the Bible is *infallible*—trustworthy and without fault in its teachings of faith and ethics. Still others hold neither view; they believe and trust some parts of Scripture, but not others.

Whatever we say we believe about the Bible, we all read Scripture selectively. Honestly, how could we not? As we've seen, the Bible is a big book of many books, written by many people over thousands of years. Even though inspired by God, it does not always speak with one voice about every subject God's people have to be concerned about.

And the biblical authors could not even have dreamed of some subjects God's people must think about today. What does the Bible say, for example, about artificial intelligence? Or climate change? Or gun regulations? Nothing directly. But it has lots to say about how human beings should use their God-given creativity, and how humans should exercise the dominion God gave them over creation, and how God's will for human beings is life. Plenty of biblical texts could be (and have been) cited to talk, even debate, about these and other subjects, but they must be *interpreted and applied* if they are to contribute to meaningful conversations.

Meaningful conversation usually happens only in meaningful relationship. A meaningful relationship with God and meaningful relationships with one another are goals of Christian living. The Bible is a means to those ends— an important, even indispensable tool for knowing and loving God and our neighbor. It has not been given to us so we can use it to shut down those with whom we disagree, or to provide quick and easy answers to difficult, complicated questions.

We forget sometimes, because, as those mobsters on *Star Trek* did with "The Book," we bind our Bibles in leather, gild their pages' edges, and make them look as beautiful as possible. But the Bible is a messy book—a wonderfully rich, impressively diverse, spiritually deep, *messy* book! *That's* its real beauty. And its real value lies in the way God has used it, and still uses it, to bring us to Jesus Christ.

Suggested Activities

1. Make a Bible Bookmark

Design and make a bookmark to use in your Bible, or to give someone else for use in theirs. Your bookmark could be as plain as a strip of cardstock decorated with a favorite verse of Scripture and religious symbols, or something fancier, perhaps using ribbons, yarn, or plastic canvas. (Various online craft sites offer instructions and tutorial videos.) Whichever kind you make, be sure it doesn't just sit around looking nice—give it lots of use as you read your Bible!

2. Blow Up a "Bible Balloon"

Choose a Scripture you find particularly inspiring. Using a marker, write its citation—name of the book, chapter, and verse number(s)—on an uninflated balloon. To remember that this Scripture was inspired by God, "inspire" your balloon by blowing it up and hanging it in a prominent place at home or in your youth ministry's meeting space.

3. Watch a Movie Clip

The 1960 film *Inherit the Wind* is a fictionalized version of the "Scopes Monkey Trial," in which a high school biology teacher was charged with violating a Tennessee law that banned the teaching of Darwin's theory of evolution by natural selection. The film is old and in black-and-white but well worth watching, especially the climactic courtroom exchange at about 1:28:27–1:45:49. Henry Drummond, defending the teacher, cross-examines Matthew Brady, who is prosecuting him.

- What does this scene lead you to think or feel?
- What's your opinion of Brady's defense of the Bible as God's Word?
- How would you, from your own beliefs, respond to Drummond's questioning of the Bible?
- Where do you see arguments about interpreting the Bible in today's society?

4. Donate a Bible

However they may differ in reading the Bible, all Christians agree the Bible matters. Sadly, some Christians do not have access to Bibles. Find a reputable ministry that distributes Bibles in this country or overseas—for example, the American Bible Society (www.americanbible.org) or the Gideons (www.gideons.org). Research their work and consider supporting them so that more believers may have what you probably take for granted, a personal copy of the Scriptures.

Daily Bible Readings

Day 1: Psalm 119:105-112

Psalm 119 is the Bible's longest psalm. (You'd never have guessed that, right?) An extended acrostic psalm, it is the devotional fruit of someone who clearly had a passionate love of Scripture. (Remember, for the psalm-singer this would have meant the Torah, the Hebrew Bible's first five books.) How has Scripture been a light for you? What do you do to increase your joy in reading and meditating on the Bible?

Day 2: Isaiah 40:6-8

These verses date from the end of the Babylonian Exile, when God sent the prophet Isaiah to prepare the people for a return to their homeland after decades away. What causes the prophet's initial reluctance to "call out" God's message? What makes the prophet able to overcome this reluctance? What does this promise mean for you?

Day 3: Deuteronomy 23:12-14

In *Half Truths*, Adam Hamilton explains how some late nineteenth-century American Christians used this text to argue against the use of indoor plumbing in church buildings. Do you think all parts of Scripture are equally important or equally relevant to modern life? Why or why not? If so, how do we apply other Scriptures that may seem strange to twenty-first-century readers? If not, how do we tell which parts are more important and which parts are less?

Day 4: John 1:1-5, 14

Whom does the Gospel of John identify as the Word of God? What are the qualities and characteristics of God's Word? Why does it matter that God's Word became a living, breathing person? In what sense, if any, is the Bible also God's Word?

Day 5: John 16:12-15

What is the Holy Spirit's role in revealing more truth to Jesus' followers after Jesus' death and resurrection? How have you experienced the Spirit's revealing more truth to you over time? How does the Spirit's work of continuing revelation relate to the revelation that is recorded in Scripture?

Day 6: John 20:30-31; 21:25

John the Evangelist is open about the fact that his writings don't and couldn't possibly tell us everything there is to know about Jesus. What does John say was his criterion for deciding what to include? What does John's purpose suggest about the primary purpose of Scripture overall?

5.

LOVE THE SINNER, HATE THE SIN

Why do you see the splinter that's in your brother's or sister's eye,
but don't notice the log in your own eye? How can you say to your
brother or sister, 'Let me take the splinter out of your eye,' when
there's a log in your eye? You deceive yourself! First take the log out
of your eye, and then you'll see clearly to take the splinter out of your
brother's or sister's eye.

—Matthew 7:3-5

Gather Around God's Word

Make your ways known to me, LORD; teach me your paths.
Lead me in your truth—teach it to me—because you are the God who saves me.

(Psalm 25:4-5)

Open the Bible and light a candle.

God of truth, none of us may dwell in your holy presence except by your amazing grace. May your Spirit always keep us aware of and thankful for your unmerited love toward us, that we may treat all our neighbors with love, remembering that all have sinned and all are saved by Jesus Christ alone. Amen.

Sing or read "Amazing Grace" (John Newton, 1779)

Jesus said … "You are truly my disciples if you remain faithful to my teaching. Then you will know the truth, and the truth will set you free." (John 8:31-32)

Jesus [said], "I am the way, the truth, and the life. No one comes to the Father except through me." (John 14:6)

Getting Started

Read the Scriptures cited below. Each illustrates one of the Seven Deadly Sins (a traditional catalogue of vices, most prevalent in Roman Catholicism, that are referenced by Adam Hamilton in *Half Truths*). Find the name of the sin in the word search and write it next to the corresponding Scripture. (An answer key appears at the end of this chapter—on your honor, no peeking!)

Genesis 4:3-8
Luke 12:15-21
1 Corinthians 11:21-22
2 Samuel 11:2-5
Daniel 4:28-33
Proverbs 24:30-34
1 Kings 21:1-4

```
W P X I C L Z E Q I S J F U A Q H J V O M L
T R G J A J C D W S L V X N N Z H P Y C O B
D I H Y L M T E V E O D G Z O Z F G R G E M
E I X X P V P E B I T H B R Y B H L Y I R P
J O Q U L B U R W X H C W N N E Q G J I D Z
S M X M C Q W G Q W F K M N O B M F T Y G E
G H S Z S B T K M H W M T C T O P W T S U L
W R A T H Y F D R C Y B I L T J B J I E P W
B G O A N Y V L A O M O R I U J V M J B I O
K Y V H B U D G U Q B D M J L C M L J G W K
G Y P D K C I M A Z L E B N G K N I W I X Z
N Q V O S P Y V N E H E I R X R Y N X B M Z
M W P A X D C I M P C R N M S W L E R N K Q
```

Study the Scripture

Read Matthew 7:1-5.

- Why does Jesus say we should not judge others?
- What exaggerated image might Jesus use today, instead of splinters and logs in people's eyes, to make the same point he originally made?
- Does Jesus' warning against passing judgment on others mean we can never say anybody's actions are wrong or sinful? Why or why not?

Read and Reflect

Everyone Else a Sinner?

The last half truth we're looking at in this study reminds me of my favorite church joke. (Well, it's not *actually* my favorite. My actual favorite is about a big, shaggy Saint Bernard who reads the Bible. But that's a different story.)

Pastor John was a preacher whose favorite themes were sin and judgment. Week in and week out, he preached about how terrible the world had become, how angry God was, and how desperately everyone in his congregation needed to shape up and repent!

And week in and week out, as Pastor John's parishioners filed out of worship, one man, Frank, would shake Pastor John's hand, look him square in the eye, and say, "You *sure* told 'em today, Reverend!" Frank never thought anything Pastor John preached about applied to *him*.

Frank's apparent apathy in the face of God's wrath drove Pastor John *crazy*. But Pastor John had made it his personal mission to save Frank's soul. He was determined to preach a sermon that would make it clear that Frank, too, was a sinner.

One winter Sunday, a huge blizzard blew into town. Nobody could make it to church—except Pastor John and Frank. Pastor John saw his big chance and seized it. He preached his most fiery sermon to a congregation of one. He pounded the pulpit and thumped his Bible with all his might. Sweat and tears poured down his face as he appealed to Frank—the only person in the pews—to repent, for the time was at hand!

The sermon ended. Pastor John went to the back of the sanctuary, as always. Frank gathered up his coat, walked up to Pastor John, shook his hand, looked him square in the eye and said: "Well...if they'd 've been here, you *sure* would've told 'em today, Reverend!"

I think the joke perfectly captures the pitfall at the heart of the statement, "Love the sinner, hate the sin." This half truth sounds innocent enough, even theologically correct. What could be wrong with hating sin? Who could argue against loving sinners? But in the end, this half truth encourages us to make the same mistake both Pastor John and Frank make. It encourages us to look at all those sinners out there, conveniently overlooking the sinner who stares at us every time we look in a mirror.

Jesus' Serious Joke

Jesus enjoyed a good joke (whether or not you think my joke falls into that category). I mean, have you ever stopped to imagine what a camel squeezing through a needle's eye would look like (Mark 10:25)? Or do you remember the time Jesus told Peter that he would miraculously find the money they needed to pay their temple tax in a fish's mouth (Matthew 17:24-27)? And a lot of the characters in the stories Jesus told do some pretty funny things. What self-respecting farmer, for example, scatters his seeds willy-nilly, with an equal chance of falling on good soil or stony ground (Mark 4:3-8)?

If you want further proof that Jesus knew the value of laughter, look no further than this session's Scripture focus. Perhaps you've heard this section of Jesus' "Sermon on the Mount" so many times, it's lost its comedic punch. But take a pencil and try to draw the scene Jesus describes: someone trying to pick a tiny splinter out of someone else's eye, all the while oblivious to the wooden two-by-four sticking out of his own (Matthew 7:3-4)!

Go ahead, try to draw it. I'll wait.

Ridiculous, isn't it? I can imagine that Jesus' joke left his original audience in stitches. But, like some of today's best comedians, Jesus used humor to make a serious point. Whenever we are more concerned about people's sins than about the people themselves, we are stepping into dangerous territory.

And with the half truth "Love the sinner, hate the sin," dangerous territory is exactly where we find ourselves.

What This Half Truth Gets Right:
Sin Is Serious

It's not that sin isn't real or doesn't matter. It is, and it does. And Scripture tells us, again and again, to avoid it.

God cautions Cain, "[I]f you don't do the right thing, sin will be waiting at the door, ready to strike! It will entice you, but you must rule over it" (Genesis 4:7). Unfortunately, Cain went on to kill Abel anyway.

- The sages of ancient Israel warn, "The path of the wicked is like deep darkness; they don't know where they will stumble" (Proverbs 4:19).
- "Avoid every kind of evil," writes the Apostle Paul (1 Thessalonians 5:22). It doesn't get much plainer than that.

Paul, in fact, may be the biblical author with the most to say about sin. For Paul, "sin" is more than an individual's "bad deed." Yes, we commit sins, but sin is a spiritual power that enslaves humanity. Sin is a mysterious, corrupting, cosmic influence that none of us can fully resist, no matter how hard we try. We're all like Cain: at one time or another we've been enticed by sin and have fallen into its clutches. "All have sinned and fall short of God's glory," Paul teaches (Romans 3:23)—and the "wages" (the result) of sin, is death (Romans 6:23).

Given this serious situation, can we afford to ignore sin, as Frank in my joke seems to? Or to pretend that whatever anyone wants to do is fine, so long as they're sincere in their desire to do it? Or to treat sin as "no big deal," or to act as though there are no objective standards of right and wrong? Of course not. Sin is toxic. Sin ruins relationships, destroys our well-being, wastes our resources, and offends our pure and holy God.

We should all follow Paul's instructions to his protégé, the young pastor Timothy: to run away from the temptation of sin and instead to "pursue righteousness, holy living, faithfulness, love, endurance, and gentleness" (1 Timothy 6:11).

What This Half Truth Gets Wrong: Neighbors, Not "Sinners"

The problem with this half truth is standing in judgment on other people as sinners.

Don't misunderstand: everyone is a sinner. But as soon as Paul states this truth in Romans, in his very next breath, he says, "all are treated as righteous freely by [God's] grace because of a ransom that was paid by Christ Jesus" (Romans 3:24). And as soon as Paul claims that the wages of sin is death, he immediately says, "God's gift is eternal life in Christ Jesus our Lord" (6:23).

When it comes to sin and salvation, everyone is on a level playing field. None of us stands a chance against sin on our own. All of us depend on God's saving grace, freely given in Jesus.

That means we can't be like Pastor John in my joke—always accusing, scrutinizing, judging others as sinners so that we can oh so generously love them in spite of their sins. As Adam Hamilton points out in *Half Truths*, not even Jesus ever commanded his followers to "love sinners"—although Jesus did in fact love sinners throughout his earthly ministry. Instead, Jesus commanded, "You must love your neighbor as you love yourself" (Matthew 22:39, quoting Leviticus 19:18).

Do you see the difference? If I approach you as a sinner, I set myself up as better than you. But if I approach you as a neighbor—as a fellow human being who is also loved by God and for whom Jesus also died—then we can have a real relationship. We can see in each other's lives how God's Spirit is constantly at work to make us both holy, as God is holy.

Finally, Adam Hamilton gives us one last thing to think about regarding this half truth. He says he's been hearing Christians talk about "loving the sinner but hating the sin" when they discuss whether the church should welcome people who are homosexual or who are involved in same-sex relationships. Christians disagree about what loving our neighbors who are gay and lesbian looks like— but, as Hamilton says, we all can and should agree on this: "What we can see clearly, and what is unmistakable regarding God's will, is that we love. The truth in 'Love the sinner, hate the sin' stops with the first word: *Love*.[17]

Truth and Love

As we finish our study of half truths that Christians often believe but really shouldn't, I want to leave you with one of the most helpful rules I know for reading Scripture. It's from Augustine of Hippo, an early fifth-century priest and bishop and one of the most influential Christian thinkers the world has seen. In his book *On Christian Doctrine*, Augustine writes:

> Whoever, then, thinks that he understands the Holy Scriptures, or any part of them, but puts such an interpretation upon them as does not tend to build up [the] twofold love of God and our neighbor, does not yet understand them as he ought.[18]

Whenever you hear someone using Scripture in a way that doesn't seem to lead to greater love, be suspicious. Think and pray about what you're hearing. Go back to the actual words in your Bible. Use your God-given intellect and draw on your experience to make up your mind. And remember Augustine's rule: if an interpretation of Scripture doesn't lead us to love God and our neighbor more, it's more than likely a half truth at best.

And be open to having your understanding of Scripture corrected sometimes too. When it comes to loving God and neighbor, we *all* have room for growth. Thanks be to God that God doesn't wait until we've "figured it all out" to love us, to save us, and to begin making us more like Jesus! Now we know only in part; but one day, in God's good time, we will "know completely in the same way that [we] have been completely known" (1 Corinthians 13:12).

Suggested Activities

1. Study Scriptures About Sin

Reread at least one of the Bible passages cited in the word search activity. Now that you know which sin each passage illustrates, what do these passages actually teach about that sin? Using a concordance or an Internet Bible search, what other verses about this sin can you find? How can the sin be recognized? How can God's people flee from the sin? What stories does Scripture contain of people resisting this sin? Where do you see this sin as a threat in today's world or in your own life?

2. Write a Prayer of Confession

The Psalms contain many examples of prayers confessing sin. Psalm 51 is probably the most famous. Tradition tells us that King David wrote and prayed Psalm 51 to confess his sin of lusting after and being with Bathsheba (as well as the sins that flowed from it; read all of 2 Samuel 11 for the full story). After reading Psalm 51, try writing your own prayer of confession. You don't have to write it as a psalm or a poem. You don't even have to use words; your prayer might take the form of a drawing or an abstract design. Whether words or images, communicate not only your sorrow for your sins but also your trust in God's mercy and forgiveness.

3. Make and Share Friendship Bread

In the Bible, the act of "breaking bread," or eating, with someone symbolizes solidarity and community. The positive connotations of eating the same food at the same table with others are one reason Jesus' opponents criticized him as a friend of sinners (Matthew 11:19). The baking and breaking together of Amish friendship bread represents solidarity and community in a unique way, because people usually prepare it from an active starter provided along with the loaf they have been given. Recipes for making the starter and for using it to bake friendship bread are abundant online; one site you may want to visit is the Friendship Bread Kitchen (http://www.friendshipbreadkitchen.com/). Making the bread takes time—ten days, in fact!—but truly loving our neighbors takes time too. Bake and share your bread and also be sure to give a bag of starter so the bread, and the loving community it represents, can continue to spread.

4. Reflect on the Face of Love

In the movie *Dead Man Walking* (1995; rated R for language and mature themes), Susan Sarandon plays Sister Helen Prejean, a real-life nun and advocate for social justice who counsels and forms a bond with convicted killer Matthew Poncelet (played by Sean Penn) before his execution. In the last hour of his life, Matthew finally confesses to his crime. Sister Helen tells him that he has dignity: "You've done terrible things, but you are a son of God." Matthew is overwhelmed; no one has ever called him a son of God. As police guards lead Matthew to the lethal injection chamber, Sister Helen tells him to look at her when he is injected: "I will be the face of love for you." Sister Helen does more than "love the sinner, hate the sin." She recognizes and names Matthew as a fellow sinner, beloved by God and saved by grace, and she embodies that love for Matthew when he needs to feel it most.

God may call few of us to minister as Sister Helen does, but spend some time thinking and praying about these questions:

- Who has been a face of love for you?
- For whom are you—or for whom could you be—the face of God's love today, and how?

Daily Bible Readings

Day 1: Leviticus 19:17-18

Most Christians don't tend to spend much time reading Leviticus, but Jesus, a devout Jew, clearly knew its contents. How do these verses balance the tension between loving people and hating sin? Have you ever rebuked someone for a sin? What happened? What reason does God give for commanding the Israelites to love their neighbors?

Day 2: Psalm 15

If we aren't supposed to think of people as sinners but as neighbors, what do we make of the psalm-singer's statement that "someone who despises those who act wickedly" (verse 4) is fit to dwell on God's holy mountain? Do you think such an attitude has any place in holy living? Why or why not? How did Jesus treat "those who act wickedly?"

Day 3: Proverbs 4

A wise man of ancient Israel teaches his son to avoid the company of sinners. To what extent do you or can you avoid people whose behavior doesn't line up with God's path of wisdom? When, if ever, should Christians cut themselves off from people whose activities can lead them and others to a bad end?

Day 4: Mark 2:14-17

Many Jews in Jesus' day considered tax collectors among the worst of sinners. Tax collectors collaborated with the occupying Roman government, enriching themselves as they gathered money for Caesar's treasury. What defense did Jesus give to critics who questioned why he would eat with tax collectors and other "sinners" (verse 16)?

Day 5: Luke 7:36-50

Why is Simon so offended by Jesus? How does the story that Jesus tells shine light on the real problem in this situation? When have you been challenged to remember God's amazing grace toward you? What extravagant response have you given to God's forgiveness of your sin?

Day 6: Ephesians 4:30–5:2

Have you ever heard Christians angrily shouting at each other about sin, even though Ephesians 4:31 calls us to much different behavior? How do Christians deal with sin in compassionate and forgiving ways, while still taking sin seriously? What is one practical way you will "live in love, as Christ loved us" (5:2 NRSV) as a result of considering the half truths we have studied together?

Answer Key

```
W P X I C L Z E Q I  S  J F U A Q H J V O M L
T R G J A J C  D  W S  L  V X N N Z H  P  Y C O B
D I H Y L M T  E  V E  O  D G Z O Z F G  R  G E M
E I X X P V P  E  B I  T  H B R  Y  B H L Y  I  R P
J O Q U L B U  R  W X  H  C W N  N  E Q G J I  D  Z
S M X M C Q W  G  Q W F K M N  O  B M F T Y G  E
G H S Z S B T K M H W M T C  T  O P W  T S U L
 W R A T H  Y F D R C Y B I L  T  J B J I E P W
B G O A N Y V L A O M O R I  U  J V M J B I O
K Y V H B U D G U Q B D M J  L  C M L J G W K
G Y P D K C I M A Z L E B N  G  K N I W I X Z
N Q V O S P  Y V N E  H E I R X R Y N X B M Z
M W P A X D C I M P C R N M S W L E R N K Q
```

52

NOTES

1. The Heidelberg Catechism (1563), Lord's Day 9/Q&A 26; https://www
   .crcna.org/welcome/beliefs/confessions/heidelberg-catechism. © 2011, Faith
   Alive Christian Resources. This translation approved by Synod 2011 of the
   Christian Reformed Church in North America and by General Synod 2011 of
   the Reformed Church in America.

2. See George Barna, *Real Teens: A Contemporary Snapshot of Youth Culture*
   (Ventura, CA: Gospel Light Publications, 2001), 125.

3. See http://www.britannica.com/topic/Poor-Richard.

4. Joseph Stromberg, "Starving Settlers in Jamestown Colony Resorted to
   Cannibalism," Smithsonian.com, April 30, 2013; http://www.smithsonianmag
   .com/history/starving-settlers-in-jamestown-colony-resorted-to
   -cannibalism-46000815/?no-ist.

5. See Dennis Montgomery, "Captain John Smith," *Colonial Williamsburg
   Journal* (Spring 1994): http://www.history.org/foundation/journal/smith.cfm.

6. Dr. Seuss, *Oh, the Places You'll Go!* (New York: Random House, 1990), 25.

7. *The Confession of 1967* (Presbyterian Church (U.S.A.)), I.B http://www.creeds
   .net/reformed/conf67.htm.

8. See Justin Shatwell, "The Theft of the Vinegar Bible," *Yankee Magazine*, "The
   Yankee Historian" blog, December 2015; http://www.yankeemagazine.com
   /yankee-historian/the-theft-of-the-vinegar-bible#_;

9. See Abby Ohlheiser, "When 'Jesus' was 'Judas' and other pretty stupendous
   Bible typos," *The Washington Post*, February 10, 2015; https://www
   .washingtonpost.com/news/arts-and-entertainment/wp/2015/02/10
   /when-jesus-was-judas-and-other-pretty-stupendous-bible-typos/.

10. https://www.bonhams.com/auctions/22715/lot/5/.

11. Quoted in American Bible Society blog, http://news.americanbible.org/blog /entry/corporate-blog/6-pope-francis-quotes-about-the-bible.

12. *Letters from the Earth*; http://www.twainquotes.com/Bible.html.

13. Heather Webb, "A Conversation with Madeline L'Engle," *Mars Hill Review* 4 (Winter/Spring 1996): 51–65; http://www.leaderu.com/marshill/mhr04 /lengle1.html.

14. Quoted in Morgan Lee, "Seven Quotes Showing Maya Angelou's Love of the Bible and Faith," May 28, 2014; http://www.christianpost.com/news /seven-quotes-showing-maya-angelous-love-of-the-bible-and-faith-120493 /#mf54J1AOVW5qvIVQ.99.

15. *Star Trek*, "A Piece of the Action," teleplay by David P. Harmon and Gene L. Coon, originally aired January 12, 1968. http://www.imdb.com/title /tt0708412/?ref_=fn_al_tt_5.

16. From Blue Letter Bible, http://bit.ly/1mdUid2.

17. Adam Hamilton, *Half Truths* (Nashville: Abingdon Press, 2016), 162.

18. Augustine, *On Christian Doctrine*, chap. 36; http://www.newadvent.org /fathers/12021.htm.

ABOUT THE AUTHORS

ADAM HAMILTON Adam Hamilton is senior pastor of The United Methodist Church of the Resurrection in the Kansas City area with an average weekly attendance of over 10,000. It has been cited as the most influential mainline church in America. Hamilton speaks across the U.S. each year on leadership and connecting with nonreligious and nominally religious people. In 2013 the White House invited him to preach at the National Prayer Service as part of the presidential inauguration festivities. In 2016 he was appointed to the President's Advisory Council on Faith-Based and Neighborhood Partnerships.

A master at explaining questions of faith in a down-to-earth fashion, he is the author of many books including *The Journey, The Way, 24 Hours That Changed the World, Enough, Why: Making Sense of God's Will, When Christians Get it Wrong, Seeing Gray in a World of Black and White, Forgiveness, Love to Stay,* and *Making Sense of the Bible.* To learn more about Adam and to follow his regular blog postings, visit www.AdamHamilton.org.

MIKE POTEET is a freelance writer and an ordained minister in the Presbyterian Church (U.S.A.). He writes for several youth and adult Christian education resources. He teaches Sunday school in a congregation near Philadelphia, Pennsylvania, and blogs about faith and pop culture for *The Sci-Fi Christian* (www.thescifichristian.com). Follow Mike on Twitter (@WriterMPoteet).

CPSIA information can be obtained
at www.ICGtesting.com
Printed in the USA
LVHW051141120121
676095LV00002B/13